W9-BFE-623

Big Machines
Rescue!

Catherine Veitch

Heinemann
LIBRARY
Chicago, Illinois

Edited by Helen Cox Cannons and Kathryn Clay
Designed by Tim Bond and Peggie Carley
Picture research by Mica Brancic and Tracy Cummins
Production by Helen McCreath
Originated by Capstone Global Library Ltd
Printed and bound in China by Leo Paper Group

18 17 16 15 14
10 9 8 7 6 5 4 3 2 1

Cataloging-in-publication information is on file
with the Library of Congress.
ISBN 978-1-4846-0588-2 (hardcover)
ISBN 978-1-4846-0595-0 (eBook PDF)

Photo Credits

Alamy: © Dave.J.Smith/Naude, 14, 15, © david tipling, 10, 11, © Ian Patrick,
16, 17, ©imagebroker/Wolfgang Bechtold, 4, 5, © johnrochaphoto, 18, 19, 22b;
Getty Images: AFP PHOTO / JIJI PRESS, 20, 21, E+/Rich Yasick, front cover; iStock:
© Nasowas, 8, 9, 22a, back cover; NASA: 6, 7, 22d, back cover; Newscom: courtesy
of Boston Dynamics, 21; Shutterstock: Jerry Sharp, 12, 13, 22c

Contents

Some words are shown in bold, **like this.** You can find out what they mean by looking in the glossary.

Ice Breaker

Super
Big
Mighty

Size

Ice breaker ships are used for rescues in icy seas. The ship's rounded front slides on top of the ice. Its enormous weight breaks through the ice.

БНИКОВ

Super Sub

This **submarine** rescue ship saves people who are trapped under water in submarines.

IMO 7623930   SEAHORSE STANDARD
                     FREMANTLE

Super
Big
Mighty
Size

submersible

Divers reach the submarine in a **submersible.** They collect the crew and bring them back to safety.

Airport Crash Tender

Special fire engines are made just for airports. They are called airport crash tenders.

monitor

Super

Big **Mighty**

Size

A hose called a **monitor** sits on top of the vehicle. The hose sprays foam over a fire to put out the flames.

Search and Rescue Helicopter

A search and rescue helicopter carries plenty of **fuel** for faraway rescues. It can stay in the air for two to three hours.

winch

A **winch** lifts injured people up into the helicopter.

Ladder Truck

A ladder truck is a fire engine with a long ladder. Firefighters use the ladder to rescue people from tall buildings.

The longest ladder on a fire engine is about 98 feet (30 meters) long. That's about as tall as six adult giraffes standing on top of each other!

Tow Truck

A tow truck rescues vehicles that have broken down or been in crashes.

boom

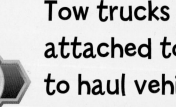

Tow trucks use a hook attached to a **boom** to haul vehicles.

Lifeboat

A lifeboat helps in an **emergency**. It rescues people from boats or from the water. Then the people are taken back to shore.

17-02

HONDA

HARBOUR MASTER

Super
Big Mighty
Size

Snow Ambulance

Two large tracks help this snow ambulance move easily over the snow.

The blade at the back clears a path in the snow.

tracks

Big Super Mighty

Size

blade

Sizing Things Up: Rescue Robots

T-53 Enryu

Height..........9 feet (2.7 meters)
Weight.........5 tons (4.5 metric tons)
Special skills ....Can lift 440 pounds
(200 kilograms)

Big Dog

Height	2.5 feet (0.76 meters)
Weight	240 pounds (109 kilograms)
Special skills	Can lift 340 pounds (154 kilograms)
	Can travel 20 miles (32 kilometers) in one day

Quiz

How much of a Machine Mega-Brain are you?
Can you match each machine name to its correct photo?

**snow ambulance • submarine rescue ship
airport crash tender • ladder truck**

1

2

3

4

Check the answers on the opposite page
to see if you got all four correct.

Glossary

boom a metal arm

emergency an unexpected, dangerous event

fuel a substance that gives power to machines

monitor a special hose on an airport fire engine

submarine a ship that can travel underwater

submersible a small craft that works underwater

winch equipment used for lifting or pulling something heavy

Find Out More

Books

Coppendale, Jean. *Fire Trucks and Rescue Vehicles*. Mighty Machines.
    Buffalo, NY: Firefly Books, 2010.

Olien, Becky. *Rescue Helicopters in Action*. Transportation Zone.
    Mankato, Minn.: Capstone Press, 2012.

Websites

http://www.emergency.qld.gov.au/aviation/aircraft/
http://pbskids.org/rogers/video_firetruck.html

Index